Do You Know How To Talk with Your Young Child?

Learn the 4 Step Approach To Converse and Connect

Dr. Suanne Lewis

SL Publishing

Dedication

This book is dedicated to two very influential folks in my life:

- Robert, my husband, who lovingly encourages my penchant for life-long learning, as well as carefully and "courageously" edits my writing, and

- Calli, the little gray curly-haired dog, who inspires me daily to be my best self. (See Story Seven)

Contents

Introduction

Welcome to our parent-to-young-child workbook. I want to be clear that this book is a book to enjoy, remember, and create warm memories of special times when talking with your child about life events.

This book is not a parenting book in the sense of understanding discipline, shaping behavior, and problem-solving. It is, instead, designed as an encouragement to approach communicating with regularity as a parenting figure with curiosity, interest, observation, a challenge to think critically, and enough courage to explore what observations of life your unique little child has!

This program is a communication program, fueled by a desire to perform our most important job as a human in a more effective way. As a social work professional recently reminded me, when parents engage in a parenting class, there may be a belief that there's a deficit, an inability to parent correctly.

If you have opened this workbook, you have the motivation to have a memorable, open, warm, and engaging relationship with your child. That speaks well of you as a parent figure, a point in your favor! You are committed to entering and participating in an expanding spiral of communication and relationship.

Today, it seems that more than ever parents and caregivers are busy coping with world issues, massive social change, fears for health and personal safety, and concerns about changes in finances and workplace situations. While all these issues are pressing on us, there is a higher demand for children's involvement in outside group activities, such as sports teams and other special interest classes. There is a pull for children to be communicating or watching online activities that parents often aren't fully aware of.

With multiple demands for children's and parents' attention, it is increasingly challenging for parents to provide the essential time and guidance in the home, once devoted to shaping and explaining the importance of positive values in our personal lives and our interaction with the world at large.

Often extended families are no longer available to share interaction, communication, and rich family stories that provide a tapestry of personal connection and communication. Shaping positive personal values has become a difficult issue given the tendency of social media to sensationalize stories of public "heroes" losing their credibility. This can give children an early sense of skepticism, pessimism, and sometimes fear.

The issues of childhood anxiety and sense of doubt have increased due to what seems to be increasing violence by seemingly disenfranchised youth, many of whom seem to feel secretive, ostracized, and isolated.

Despite or perhaps because of the great changes in our world and its social structures, we need to take some time each day to clarify and grow more comfortable with our sense of positive values. We need to help our children learn the importance of such values as love, kindness, and respect, despite the hardships they see around them.

There are other benefits to developing and maintaining an open relationship with your child based on effective communication skills. Students with involved parents have been found to have better grades and achievement test scores, attend school more regularly, have better social skills, show improved behavior, and adapt well to school.

Developmentally, children are more open to parental influence before the pre-teen and teen years. Developing an open communication relationship in which your child has learned and can discuss positive parental values and expectations is important to establish in early childhood.

Children learn from observation, so demonstrating effective and caring parental communication provides essential modeling for your child. Asking for your child's opinions and experiences and promoting their version of problem-solving encourages your child to express him or herself and builds self-understanding and confidence. This can give your child increased resilience in times of unexpected change.

Your respect for your child's opinions and experiences as an individual fosters trust in you and respect for you, which are essential as you help guide your child in his/her maturation.

Effective communication because it is reciprocal, based on openness, honesty, love, and emotional presence, causes a relationship to expand and deepen. Despite stressors, growth, differing lifestyles, disagreements, and disappointments, the relationship can endure because you have been a presence, a witness, and a co-creator of understanding and development. What an honorable role for a parenting figure!

When parents of young children take action to influence the development of positive values and open, honest communication, they ensure a more promising future for their child and the world at large.

The main topics for our work will include the following:

1. Establishing a communication "space."

2. Transitioning to relaxed listening and talking using moving and focusing techniques.

3. Learning and practicing effective communication techniques for open conversations and relationship building.

4. Using teaching stories to provide themes, language, characters, and connections for opening non-threatening discussions.

5. Adopting suggested small projects to foster planning, cooperation, increased conversation, shared success, and "living" the values discussed.

We have a lot of interesting things to do to start you and your child on an expanding spiral of communication and relationship!

Chapter 1: Establishing a Communication "Space"

Does establishing a communication "space" mean I have to find another room in my already crowded household? No. This "space" refers to a designated time and area for you and your child to converse with one another without interruption by noise, television, visitors, or cell phones (yours too, Mom) for an established time regularly. At the bare minimum this would be 20-30 minutes weekly when each of you knows you'll have time to catch up and discuss life and its issues without any distractions or intrusions.

An ideal time for this quiet communication "space" would be in the evening before bedtime. This allows time for you and your child to wind down physically from your day, to focus on just one thing (your pleasant communication), and to remain free from the stimulating light from cell phones, computers, televisions, and iPads. Each of you can relax and sleep more quickly and soundly after your special time together. Hopefully, both of you will find that you would like to establish this "space" more often.

Small reinforcements help to establish new patterns of behavior, so sharing a light snack and a small beverage (not major snacking which will detract from the purpose of making the "space"), bringing a favorite blanket to snuggle in, holding a favorite toy to share a story with, or allowing a quiet pet to attend might make this an especially "special time."

Studies have shown that an essential key to developing and consistently following through with a new desired routine or habit is to set an intention each week including the place, time of day, and the number of times per week you will complete your activity. When you finish your goal for the week, then simply set a goal for the next week. This could be a great way for you and your little one to develop a great habit of having open and important conversations with one another.

Chapter 2: Transitioning to Relaxed Listening and Talking

E ffective communication requires focus and attention. After a busy day of work, school, chores, or play, frequently we need to release physical and muscular tension before we settle down. Throughout the workbook, for each session, there will be a brief movement activity, based on complementary health techniques of yoga, qigong, or t'ai chi that help ground our physical energy and release tension in our bodies. The movements are brief and very gentle and can be done standing or seated. Not only do these simple movements begin to help us and our child relax the tension and transition to quiet time, but they also enable our child to practice reciprocal movement with us (moving as we do, based on their observation of us). This type of mirroring has been shown to help in developing trust and a sense of safety.

Our attention is enhanced by nourishing our brains with oxygen. The oxygen flow promoted by deep, slow breathing further relaxes our body while helping our brain focus attention on the present moment, releasing thoughts about what happened earlier in the day or worries about what might happen tomorrow. We will pair a simple breathing technique with our gentle movements to boost the ability to attend to stories and talking points. Pairing muscle relaxation and focused attention with being in your presence will further enhance the precious relationship you have with your child.

These gentle focus and movement techniques have been offered in some school systems to help children become better settled in class as well as to enhance pro-social behavior. Being able to slow down and pause before acting can be a very beneficial strength to have!

As we cover the step of attention or focus, it's time to clarify that familiar word "mindfulness." While we hear that word often these days, perhaps it isn't clear exactly what it means in everyday use.

When we are mindful, we are completely aware of where we are, exactly what and how we are doing, and particularly who we are with. Our attention is not lingering on other things such as where we're going next, who is texting us, what happened earlier, someone we saw this morning, or what we're planning for tomorrow, for example.

In a mindful state of being, we are acutely aware of what we are hearing, seeing, smelling, feeling, speaking, moving, and experiencing in the moment.

Do you have a memory of ever being in the presence of someone who was so engaged in being in your presence that you felt you were the only person in a room full of other people? It's a very special feeling.

When you mindfully interact with your young child, you give a very special gift to him or her. Modeling this practice for your child will be invaluable in helping him relate effectively with his environment and others as he grows and matures.

Chapter 3: Learning and Practicing Effective Communication Techniques

We talk and hear speech, but do we hear and process what someone intended to communicate? Were we clear about what we intended to say? How many times have we not "heard" what someone else told us? How many times has someone told us, "I didn't think that was what you meant!" We communicate all the time, not only with words but also with our voice tone and volume, gestures, facial expressions, posture, and internal intentions (which don't always remain invisible to sensitive others).

Researchers tell us that young children understand many words long before they can say them. By lovingly encouraging our young child to express herself while listening with acceptance and curiosity, we help her increase her vocabulary, help her to understand and express her feelings, assist her in beginning to develop opinions and ways of problem-solving, as well as encourage her to talk about any problems or discomforts she might be having. All these benefits help build confidence, not only in herself but, in you, as her parent figure, through your role-modeling, presence, and witnessing of her precious life.

Chapter 4: Using Storytelling to Provide Interesting, Non-threatening Characters and Situations

Every story we encounter teaches us something about ourselves. As Dr. Jean Houston, master storyteller, author, thought leader and principal founder of the human potential movement explains, storytelling differentiates humans from other species. Stories chronicle our history through themes, characters, ideas, and images.

What value can stories provide for our young children? Listeners engage in the story and become more open to learning. Visual learning is enhanced when the listener develops mental pictures of the characters, scene, and plot being described. Auditory learning takes place with the use of words, descriptions, voice tone, and rhythm.

Emotional learning is stimulated as the listener relates to the thoughts and feelings of the characters and situations.

Stories have multiple meanings that can be discovered and discussed. They help us understand ourselves and help us make sense of the world without being as threatened or challenged as coping with real-life situations. Stories help us create connections among people and other creatures, as well as the world at large. We engage in storytelling and listening every day: reminiscing, gossiping, reading books and the news, watching television, or engaging in video games.

As a young child, I remember the importance of hearing stories from my grandmother, parents, and extended family members. Those stories, though not always about themselves, but by the choices of their subject matter, gave me a sense of my family members. Their stories illustrated my family's expectations of me and the place that we all played in the world in terms of our interactions, behaviors, and how we might best get along. Of course, as anyone who knows me well would agree, my favorite stories were about animals.

One memory I recall from my early childhood is about my short, busty, stout grandmother, who lived next door to me. She was a very quiet woman who wore long cotton house dresses, typically an apron, and heavy stockings with clunky black shoes. She always had a steel gray bun pulled back during the day and had almost waist-length hair when she took it down to brush it at night. I used to "escape" from my house in the afternoons looking for my grandmother's cat who avoided my over-exuberance at all costs. When I got to my grandmother's back door, she greeted me quietly and led me through the house to sit on the front porch with her on a large swing overlooking hollyhocks that I always thought looked like dancing ladies.

My grandmother sat rocking the swing in the rhythm of my heartbeat it seemed, holding the striped cat on her lap as she stroked it firmly along its entire body. As she swung and stroked, the cat and I calmed and listened to her tell the stories of her childhood, using Welsh words like "flibbertigibbet" and "cattywampus" until the cat and I were comfortable, ensconced in the quiet, constant love of this precious woman whom we loved right back. My grandmother, a simple and largely uneducated woman, practiced the four essential aspects of holding important conversations with a young child: relax, focus, communicate, and connect!

In my adult life as a busy, working, divorced mother of a young son, I felt sometimes that I was treading water, hoping that no one was drowning. With the support of my two retired parents, however, who were steady, stable, and loving adults, I was fortunate to have the opportunity to spend regular time reading and talking with my son, particularly in the evenings. Our mutual love of good stories, either fiction or real life, gave us great opportunities for discussing our unique perspectives on the outcomes.

My son is a mid-life adult now. We have different lifestyles and don't see each other often, but usually talk with each other every day. We still share our interest in books and stories about humans and animals. These stories continue to give us characters, images, themes, and ideas that we share regularly. It gives us a chance to discuss actions we have taken, and those we have chosen not to. Through our discussions, we know each other well, understand our differences, and have enjoyed having the opportunity to grow in understanding the values we each have in our lives.

I hope my teaching stories about animal characters and their places in the natural world, which also is changing radically, will help you and your children take some time to enjoy one another, feel the love that lives among you, and consider some positive ways of interacting with our changing environment.

CHAPTER 5: DEVELOPING SMALL PROJECTS TO BRING STORIES TO LIFE

Planning a project (albeit small) about one of the stories in the lessons can be positive in many ways. Creating a picture, taking an action, or demonstrating a gesture such as a "thank you" brings abstract learning into the concrete everyday world of applying what has been learned. This is a powerful tool for kinesthetic learners, those who learn by doing.

Planning between you and your child requires a bit of cooperation, such as deciding what to do, getting materials together, and considering actions that would be appropriate, all of which fosters the development of critical thinking (planning, setting steps to take, paying attention, and following through). Small steps such as these prepare your little one to face the great big world eventually. What good work!

Notice through the book that if you and your child decide to work on a small project after considering a story, you "earn bonus points" or "extra credit." This refers to the idea that when you engage in a voluntary project together you both win at building your relationship and communication together!

Chapter 6: What Are the Essentials of Communication

Communication takes place constantly around us even if we're unconscious of it happening. Lots of it is ineffective. How do I mean this?

If, as research suggests, 90% of all communication is non-verbal, we are sending messages to those around us with our posture, facial expression, sighs, voice tone, and gestures as we talk on the phone, to someone else near us, or to our pet. Those who observe us, often our young child who is far more aware than we might imagine, make assumptions about how we feel and what we are trying to communicate to them. Consider the stories you know about children of divorced parents who believe the divorce is their fault!

Being more conscious of the principles of effective communication will help clarify the messages we send and prevent some misinterpretation. We won't make it perfect, but we can certainly make it better!

Here are some important principles of communication:

- Effective communication has both a sender and a receiver.

- When we intend to communicate our message, we know who the receiver is and frame the message in a way we wish the receiver to understand us.

- We monitor our non-verbals, so they accurately tell the listener or receiver how we feel and want to express ourselves.

- We give the receiver a chance to tell us what they "heard." In other words, we make sure the message was received as we intended, and we check for their understanding. This process is a two-way process. We let our children know what we think we heard them express, allowing them to correct us if we misunderstood.

- If the receiver misunderstood, we clarify the message. For our young child, we do this in a patient, clear way. This is a teaching moment for learning vocabulary, paying attention, and not making assumptions. Your child will also learn that having conversations is a two-way process, something that will help both of you in the future, particularly as s/he reaches adolescence and may be inclined to disengage a bit.

- I like to think of working on effective communication as providing an "expanding spiral of communication and relationship."

What does that fancy concept mean? Simply this: as we learn and teach our child how to have a genuine exchange of communication back and forth between us, we grow in our understanding and trust of one another. That doesn't mean we always agree, but we trust that we are honest individuals and honor that we're each trying to be understood. We are each present to the other. That's a pretty good basis for a close relationship! That increasing openness and understanding can help us develop an ever-greater respect for one another and our individuality.

CHAPTER 7: REVIEW

Let's review our 4 essential steps for talking with our young children (4stepsconnect)

- Relax by stretching out those muscles tensed by our activities and challenges of the day, such as exercise, play, worry, and work.

- Focus attention by slowly supplying oxygen to our bodies and brain through long deep breathing, avoiding attention interruptions for a specified time, and setting an intention to pay attention.

- Communicate using effective communication techniques.

- Engage in a conversation using interesting stories allowing your child to express opinions, wonder, and even plan ways to bring the ideas in the stories to life.

Chapter 8: Opening Conversation Basics

Our major goal is to begin to have open conversations with our young child that hopefully will continue through our relationship as each of us grows older.

A good place to start in this chapter as we learn to employ our 4-step approach is to remember two simple directions.

Avoid asking "yes" or "no" questions. If you do ask one of these, often, you will simply get one-word answers. This often happens with young children, someone who is feeling defensive, or a person who is not paying much attention.

That isn't what you're looking for and it can be frustrating. Don't worry, I'll give you many examples of open-ended style questions in our 'talking points' after each story.

Avoid asking "why" questions when possible. "Why" questions can seem judgmental and might put your young child on the defensive, which can shut down any further discussion or cause him to become argumentative, trying to defend his position. Sometimes we have a natural reaction, particularly an emotional one, and we can't say why we have it. Exploring with open-ended statements and questions, such as, "Try to tell me more about that." "How did you feel at the time?" can provide an opening for better understanding on your part, and keener self-awareness on your child's part, avoiding that apparent need to justify his or her point of view.

In a description in her virtual class on "Quantum Powers," Jean Houston made an interesting point about a classic children's book, The Little Prince. In the story, the Little Prince says about grown-ups: "When you tell them that you have made a new friend, they never ask you any questions about essential matters. They never say to you, 'What does his voice sound like? What games does he love best? Does he collect butterflies?' Instead, the Little Prince describes grown-ups' questions as asking about the friend's age, how much his father makes, and other unimportant topics.

It's important to consider, what are the "essential" matters in your child's life, or in anyone else's you are learning to know. What are the meaningful thoughts, feelings, hopes, and experiences that make them unique? Be open to the new and the interesting!

In this chapter, we're going to have two simple stories. One presents the issue of "peacefulness" and the other "gratitude." The stories throughout the book are vignettes, that present characters and a situation about a life value that might be interpreted in different ways. The stories aren't designed to be moralistic but, instead, are intended to provide you and your child the opportunity to talk about what is important to you both and how you would think, feel, or act in those situations. In that way, the stories can give you a way of discussing the values again in the future by recalling and referring to the characters and storylines that are already familiar to you.

***

Preparing for your quiet time with your child
Get Ready for Story One

Releasing physical tension: Roll slowly across the soles of your feet, rolling from your heel to the ball of your foot, then reversing, rolling from the ball of your foot to your heel. This can demand a bit of concentration. An easy way to do this is to bend your knees softly as you roll. Straighten your knees after you roll forward, then bend and straighten again when you roll back. You can repeat this slowly a few times.

Adaptation: If you or your child are unable to do this release of tension while standing, it can be done by sitting up in a chair with feet flat on the floor and rolling forward and back across the balls of your feet in that way.

Why does this work to release tension? Briefly, you have acupressure points on the bottoms of your feet that when pressed release tension in various parts of your body. We take our feet for granted. We often don't even think that our feet work hard for us as well as have important connections to the energy channels in our bodies.

Focusing attention: Breathe deeply down into your tummy. You can let your tummy expand as you breathe slowly and deeply into it. When it is full of oxygen, slowly release your breath from the top of your chest back down to your belly. You can squeeze your tummy in. This full breath provides your brain with oxygen, clears your lungs, releases more tension in your body, and helps you to be focused and calm. You can take a few slow breaths like that to settle in.

***

Mr. Toad Moves to the Neighborhood Teaching Tale (Peacefulness, Love, and Good Intentions)

Mr. Toad arrived in the neighborhood late one night, quietly and with little luggage, only a small backpack containing a toothbrush and a change of shoes. (It gets quite muddy sitting in flower beds much of the time.)

Calli, the curly-haired dog who lives in The House, noticed him first. He was tucked in close to the back porch step and she greeted him with a snoot each time she went out on a "business trip."

Bob, the man who lives in The House, said "Good morning" to the toad as he was packing the car for a family vacation. Mr. Toad returned a quiet greeting and introduced himself as "Theo." Theo was quite stocky and built close to the ground. If asked by a police artist to describe him, it would be difficult, because he was a creature who blended in very well with his surroundings, particularly the rough, brown mulch in the flower bed.

When Bob, trying to start a conversation, asked where Theo was from and why he relocated to The House, he responded simply, "I'm here to serve." Not knowing quite what to say to that, Bob responded simply in return, "Hmmm...."

Theo, reluctant to cause hard feelings, and wanting to avoid any suspicion about his intentions, explained, "The world is in great need of peacefulness, goodwill, and acceptance. I hope that you will accept me with my stocky build, warts, bumps, and bulgy eyes. In exchange, I will quietly guard your house against pests, provide you companionship, and sit peacefully in your garden with kindness, love, and good intentions."

Bob, who is usually a talkative sort, was struck with Theo's humility and sincerity, and merely responded, "Thank you. I accept!"

Mr. Toad Talking Points: (Use all or a few of the talking points. You might use some and if you read the story again, use others, or simply choose which ones make the most sense to you and your child)

- How is Mr. Toad different from many story characters or people you know?

- What seemed to surprise Bob about his talk with Theo?

- In our world, many people are encouraged to be busy, and active, and "don't waste time." What other instructions have you heard? "Speak louder"? "Take part"? "Join in"? "Hurry up"? (Often being busy and quick is seen as more positive than being quiet and taking our time.)

- Whom do you know who is peaceful? When are good times to be peaceful? Choose two: At a sporting event; when others in your house are still sleeping; when someone is trying to hear or say an important message; or in a library.

- How does Mr. Toad look? Sometimes it can be difficult to like someone who is not attractive.

- What are things to look for in caring for someone besides

being attractive?

- Whom do you know who is peaceful, who is a good companion, and who is kind and has good intentions? I wonder what it would be like to be that way.

For a few "extra credit points" for parent and child: Is there a goal you would like to practice in the next few days that has to do with being peaceful, accepting of others, being kind, or sharing good intentions? Being quiet when others are talking? Smiling or saying "hello" to someone who doesn't seem very popular? Drawing a picture of Mr. Toad?

***

Next is Story Two

Deirdre and Dawn Teaching Tale (Gratitude)

Maggie sat outside basking in the summer weather with the sound of the little waterfall behind The House, and the smell of the Norwegian Spruce trees shading the back yard. She heard the robin's call in the spruce tree and the buzz of bees around the lavender growing nearby. Busy natural sounds seemed to make the yard a safe oasis, a place of rest. As she inhaled the fragrant air, she felt a presence nearby, and eyes focused on her. Looking up from the book she was enjoying, she spotted a beautiful grown female deer standing with a lovely spotted fawn.

The three of them passed what seemed like several minutes gazing into each other's eyes. Cautiously, Maggie smiled and spoke in a soft voice, "Hello, I'm glad to see you're back. Please stay a while. You're safe here with me."

The doe spoke softly in response, "Hello dear lady. I feel the quiet safety and caring you bring to this lovely spot. I am Deirdre and I want to thank you for giving Dawn a safe, quiet place to rest and drink when I'm out looking for food and a safe bed for us to hide in for the night. These yards lie on an old game trail through the mountains, but now, new houses cover much of the area our deer friends have used for running and grazing for many years. We don't have a lot of space to live safely with all the fences, lawnmowers, hunters, and four-wheelers around. Please know that I appreciate your care and respect. Sometimes humans don't realize that other creatures feel gratitude, but I think it's an important emotion to feel and especially to express."

As Maggie felt a lump in her throat and tears gather at the corners of her eyes, she responded, "I'm humbled by your trust and your comments, and hope that you, your family, and I can share this beautiful place safely together for a long time to come." As she looked up, she saw that Deirdre and her fawn had faded away suddenly and silently, and she was alone in her backyard again.

Deirdre and Dawn Talking Points:

- What are you grateful for?

- When have you thanked someone for what they've done for you or given you?

- How did it feel to do that?

- How does it feel when someone thanks you?

- What did you think about Deirdre? What about Maggie?

For a bonus for mom and child: Is there a goal you might think of for the next few days to practice being grateful? Thanking someone for being kind to you, thinking of how you might make your house or yard safe for a wild creature, drawing a picture of Deirdre or Dawn?

You've completed the first set of stories and talking points!! I hope you enjoyed them and even took the challenge to work on a small project together.

CHAPTER 9: USING YOUR BODY TO LISTEN

We don't just listen with our ears. When we are communicating effectively, we listen with our whole bodies, and listening with our bodies builds trust. If we are paying attention, we hear 10% of the verbal communication and observe the other 90% that is non-verbal. That's good stuff!

- Use your eyes: Look at your little one when you are having conversations. Observe nervous movements, energy levels, or changes in facial expression, for example.

- Use your posture: Lean toward your child when listening. Being relaxed is good but be sure to indicate that you're alert and interested.

- Use your voice: Use a warm, gentle voice tone, but speak clearly so your child will hear and understand.

- Use your heart: Listen with love, interest, and curiosity about this unique person you're with. Let this love shine in your eyes.

- Use your nose: Does your child have healthy "little one" smells, for example: of soap, activity, and the out of doors? Do you notice an odor of nerves or illness?

- Use touch and space: Be close if that feels safe to both of you. A hug or a handhold can be nice.

***

Get Ready for Story Three

Releasing Physical Tension: Side stretches or Half Moon Pose--Raise one arm at a time and stretch (raise the left arm and stretch it over your head if you can reach easily leaning to the right, feeling a stretch on the left side). Follow through now with raising the right arm and stretching your right side as you lean to the left. You can do this a few times alternating arms. If either you or your child feels stiff, start with small stretches to warm up and gradually increase the stretch if this feels comfortable. If this movement is impossible for you, sit and simply lengthen each side of your body allowing some stretch and lengthening in each side. Remember to move cautiously and check with your physician if you have questions about any movements suggested in the book.

Focusing attention: Try a few slow, deep breaths, raising your arms slowly on an inhale and lowering your arms slowly on a long exhale.

***

Nellie and Mags Teaching Tale (Friendship)

On a gently rolling hillside near The House, there is a sunny pasture with a small stream running along the base of it. It is dotted with a few small shade trees nearby.

As a plump black and white Holstein cow ambled along the top of the hill on the path coming from The Barn, a large brown Guernsey cow, with a white underbelly and white star on her forehead gave a friendly, "Moo...". Miss black-and-white, Nellie, responded with her own, "Moo!" and picked up her pace as she moved to the brown heifer, named Mags. Nellie and Mags greeted each other with more sounds and a touch of their soft velvety noses, finally shifting close together.

Mags started the conversation, "Nellie, it's so good to see your beautiful black and white spots come out of the barn. Your spots seem friendly, and they make me smile. You're cheerful looking and when you come to the pasture, I feel cheerful too!"

"Ah, that's so nice of you to say, Mags," Nellie responded. "I feel happy to see you too, but for different reasons. Your soft brown hair and that wonderful star on your forehead make me feel peaceful. I always look forward to our quiet days with each other and know that you'll be friendly and understanding as we have our lunch together."

Nellie said to Mags as they both swatted flies casually with their tails, "I heard the farmer telling his helper that cows that are called by their names produce a lot more milk than those cows who are not named. I don't believe that. I think it's the friendships we have with one another that make us happy, relaxed, feeling loved, and useful. Having good friends helps us to be the very best of who we're meant to be. Seeing you every day, spending time with you, telling you what's on my mind, and knowing that you are listening is very important to me."

"I know what you mean, Nellie," Mags responded. "With a good old friend like you, I feel noticed, recognized, and important in the world. Even though we're different in lots of ways, standing with you, cooling our feet and legs in the stream, or chatting about the day under one of the trees in the field is the best part of the day. We encourage one another to feel good about ourselves."

Hearing the farmer's call and noticing the lateness of the day, the two good friends turned slowly to head back up through the field. Their big hips swayed from side to side as they bumped each other's shoulders and quietly "mooed" to one another in complete under-standing and affection.

Nellie and Mags Talking Points:

- What lets you know that Mags and Nellie are friends? (Greeting? Liking talking to each other? Being close?)

- How are Nellie and Mags the same and how are they differ-ent?

- How is it nice to be friends with someone different from you?

- How is it nice to be friends with someone who is the same as you?

- Do you have a friend who is different from you? How they look? Where they are from? Other ways they are different?

- Do you have a friend who is very much the same as you? How are you the same?

- When is it especially nice to be with a friend?

- When are times when it is difficult to be a friend?

- How can you remain a friend even in those hard times?

- Have you had times when you decided that someone was not a person who was good for you to be friends with? If so, how did you handle it?

Friends can be important to us, giving us comfort and support, and being concerned about us when others might not notice we're having a hard time. Friends also can give us chances to take part in different activities we wouldn't know about.

For a bonus for parent and child: Over the next few days, how can you celebrate having a good friend? Thinking about the differences between you that you like? Thinking about what you like to do together? Telling your friend that you're glad to be friends? Greeting your friend with a smile? What other ways were you thinking of?

Chapter 10: Exploring Thoughts and Feelings

All of us need to learn the difference between thoughts and feelings. Thoughts can create feelings of stress sometimes. They can be the result of learning that's not accurate and might need to be challenged. This can occur when we experience something and jump to conclusions about why it happened and what it means. For example, you tell your child to stay away from the stove and not to touch a pot, but she's curious and wants to help Mommy. She burns two fingers and immediately assumes that she got burned because she is a "bad girl," because she disobeyed. The reason she got burned is that pots get hot when the stove is turned on. You knew this and wanted to protect her because you love her, but your little one might remember that she was punished (burned) because she didn't do as she was told. This occurrence distorts her thinking and causes her to feel inadequate, "remembering" that she was punished for being "bad" in the past. Can you see the difference between rational and irrational thinking as well as understand how complicated thoughts and feelings can become?

An adult example of distorted thinking which is often constructed by our personal history or cultural experiences (referred to as limiting beliefs) would be our tendency to "catastrophize," believing that the world is just waiting to make something bad happen to us. We might have learned as young children that we shouldn't be too optimistic and risk being disappointed. For the most part, however, life happens, both good and bad. And, in truth, we often have more good fortune if we look for the positive possibilities in life.

Feelings are personal and are often associated with bodily reactions. We get "butterflies" in our gut when we feel anxious. We notice that our body gets tense when we are scared. When we feel sad, we might get tightness in our throat or chest, or feel that we need to go to bed and cover our heads. Feelings aren't rational. They often are very important in prompting us about how to respond to the world. For example, anger might be prompted by someone else violating our trust or our personal space. Anger could sometimes be associated with anger at ourselves for being disappointing in some way. These examples of anger warn us to be alert and establish some limits or boundaries for others and ourselves.

Joy is a feeling that might prompt us to be active, reach out to others, and express ourselves in loving ways. It often results from experiencing positive attention, noticing beautiful sights or sounds, and feeling healthy and well-rested, for example.

Feelings are individual reactions to situations, events, and inter-actions. If we explore our child's feelings in various situations or as they are related to story situations, we can learn a lot about our child's personality, coping strategies, and vulnerabilities. It is powerful to understand how our child feels, and it is very important to resist discounting those feelings or prohibiting certain feelings from being expressed. As parents, we need to understand and sometimes develop guidelines for how our child's feelings as well as our own are best expressed to the world.

***

Get Ready for Story Four

Release Physical Tension: Relax your body. Standing if you can, release your arms, and simply bounce on your feet, allowing your knees to soften and straighten as you bounce. Smile and allow yourself to have a fun time. If you're unable to stand, allow your trunk, arms, and legs to relax and bounce your knees up and down.

Focusing Your Attention: Let's do Mountain Pose! "Plant" your feet not quite hip-width apart, or if seated, simply place them under your knees. Bring your arms down to your sides and stand or sit as if you are a tall mountain. Inhale slowly from the earth (your roots) up through your body, then exhale slowly down through the soles of your feet. Do this a few times.

***

Bertha Bear and Bruin Teaching Tale (Responsibility)

Sasha looked out the window of The House and saw the birdfeeder and the hook on which it was placed. It was mangled and dangling at a crazy angle. Sasha was puzzled and went out to see what had happened.

The damage was too great to have been done by just the wind. Both the hook and bird feeder were beyond fixing. Most of the bird food (pieces of fruit, seeds, and suet) was gone, with just a few remaining seeds spilled on the ground. Neighborhood birds were chittering in the trees, talking about the damage and the lack of readily available food. What could have happened?

It was a late October day and was beginning to become dusk. Sasha noticed some dogs barking in the area and looked up to see two large, dark animals approaching. He quietly stood his ground trying to determine if the animals were large, unfamiliar dogs, or possibly black bears. They both approached slowly and cautiously. Sasha's heart rate increased, and he felt a chill as he realized they were two bears. The large female, as she got closer, stopped, and spoke to him in quiet, but firm tones.

"I'm Bertha and this is my young son, Bruin. You seem to have noticed that your bird feeder was destroyed. I would like you to know that Bruin did that while out wandering about in the area, and I've encouraged him to come to admit his responsibility for the damage."

Bruin, a bit smaller and ganglier than his mother, quickly jumped in, "I'm sorry I ruined your feeder! I was out walking around and got hungry for a snack. I didn't mean to cause any trouble for you.

Mom made me come talk to you. I'm sorry!" After all those comments, Bruin stopped and seemed to need to catch his breath, with a puff through his long fuzzy nose.

Sasha was stunned by the interaction and simply said, "Oh, I see."

Bertha again firmly chimed in, "Young ones make mistakes until they learn to live in the world without harming other people and their property. But it's my responsibility to teach them to take good care of themselves, to avoid putting themselves in harm's way, and not to damage what's around them, either other creatures or their property. I'm sorry we created trouble for you."

Regaining some sense of calm, Sasha spoke up, "I appreciate your honesty and your sense of duty. But I could take some responsibility here too. How about if I don't put the bird feeders out until you and your families are resting through the winter? That way I won't be tempting your young ones to stop for a 'snack'."

The two bears nodded, turned towards the woods, and loped with thick dark fur rippling over their large backs and leg muscles. In moments they were out of sight in the deepening darkness.

Sasha took a deep breath he seemed to be holding, and retreated to the house, taking the ruined bird feeder with him.

Bertha Bear and Bruin Talking Points:

We all make mistakes, and the bonus of that is we can learn how not to make them again. Taking responsibility for what we do is important. It helps us to learn, keeps others from being blamed for our mistakes, and might help others to learn better how to get along. Parents, it is important to use some of the questions that explore both feelings and thoughts.

Helping others to get along better might be to remove temptations from others who might take advantage of our carelessness. How? Lock your car doors; don't display valuables in your car; put away your bike, skateboard, tools, or other valued items you left out in the yard.

- If you were Bruin's mother, what would you do? · How did you think Bruin handled the situation?

- How do you think Sasha felt when he saw the bears coming? Worried? Afraid?

- How would you feel?

- What was Sasha thinking? Wondering what he should do? Yell? Be mean?

- What do you think Bruin thought was going to happen? How did he feel?

- How about Sasha? What decision would you make if you were Sasha?

- How did you feel when you made a mistake in the past? Embarrassed? Concerned that you might be punished? What did you think about it

For a bonus for mom and child: What could you do in the next few days to take responsibility for something you're asked to do or something you have already done? Pick up your coat and hang it? Say "I'm sorry," if you did something that bothered someone else? Draw a picture of Bruin and the bird feeder? Put away things your dog might chew on? Anything else?

CHAPTER 11: COPING WITH OTHERS IN THE MIX

As young children experience others in school, groups, or other social interactions, it can be confusing and challenging to be confronted with unexpected reactions. These reactions can be from others or even from themselves!

Two of these situations that are important to be aware of and understand are: being on one side of jealousy or the other and feeling discounted and unheard. To work on understanding these issues, we're next going to work on stories about accepting one's gifts or talents and developing an assertiveness technique. Both can be important for building self-confidence as well as coping well in new situations.

***

Get Ready for Story Five

Release Physical Tension: Let's try Rocking Motion! In a standing position or seated, if necessary, we're going to roll across the soles of our feet from heel to the balls of our feet while holding our arms down and then gently swinging our arms forwards, with palms up. Then gently swing your arms back with palms facing behind you as you roll toward your heels. Repeat this movement slowly forward and back several times. Again, to make this a bit easier you can bend your knees slightly then straighten as you arrive on the balls of your feet, then bend your knees slightly and straighten as you arrive on your heels. Look ahead to help you with your balance if necessary.

Focusing Attention: Let's stand like a tall tree. Press the palms of your hands together over your head, or as close as you comfortably can. Place one heel against the ankle of your opposite leg and balance there. You can place most of your weight on one leg for a few moments and then shift to the other leg for a change. If this isn't possible, simply balance with your weight on both legs, focusing your attention on your pressing palms. Be sure to breathe fully and deeply up from your belly, then down through the soles of your feet.

***

Barney Celebrates His Life! Teaching Tale (Recognizing Your Talent)

Sam was sitting on the small dock overlooking the lake at The House. He was focused on whether he had any true friends. Sam had gotten a perfect grade on a quiz that day and when the teacher mentioned it during class some of his classmates gave him ugly looks. Another "friend" wouldn't sit with him on the bus ride home because Sam was chosen for a fun part in a class play. Sam was lost in feeling confused and hurt. What had he done wrong?

Just at that moment, a bright object caught his eye and in the next moment he heard what he thought was a roaring sound in his ear. He re-focused and saw a brilliant large dragonfly with an iridescent green head and blue body hovering in front of him. It flew high then came down low again, moving backward, forwards, and sideways, while the sun shimmered and played off the smooth surface of the lake. As the dragonfly was performing his aerial tricks, Sam asked him his name and grumpily asked why he was keeping so close to him.

"My name's Barney, and I think you need my advice!" Sam just looked at him and smiled. After all, he was a young boy who lived in a nice place and had a mom and grandparents who took good care of him. Why would he need the help of a large bug, even if he was iridescent and flew like a miniature helicopter?

Barney wasn't the least bit put off by Sam's skeptical grin. He performed a few more flying tricks, then settled back at Sam's eye level.

"It took me a while, but I've found that I have some terrific talents that not many other creatures in my crowd have! My gifts feel wonderful and thrilling to me when I use them. When I am pleasing myself by doing the things I know I can do and even improve with practice, sometimes it bothers others who are less talented. It makes them a little jealous; they grumble a bit, you know?" Sam nodded his understanding but said nothing.

"But you see, Sam, I have come to understand myself and what I can do. When I follow through on my special skill and talent, I celebrate my life to its fullest at that moment. I like myself and it gives those around me permission to like themselves too. We're all unique--no sense in comparing. That's what makes life interesting; it's a little bit like a three-ring circus and I can be one of the stars!"

Barney Celebrates His Life Talking Points:

- Who is your favorite character in the story? What do you like about him?

- What are Barney's special talents?

- What makes Barney seem so happy?

- What seemed to make Sam think he didn't have any true friends? I wonder if his friends were jealous that he was doing well that day. What do you think?

- Try to think of someone you know who does something better than you do. How do you feel about that?

- What can you do very well?

Sometimes when we can do something well, we think it's "no big deal" even if others can't do it as well as we can. It's okay if we are happy that we can do something better than others can. How do we do that without seeming to be bragging?

For a special bonus for parent and child:

Breathe in deeply, think for a moment (both parent and child), smile, and say out loud, "I am good at ______________________!" If you need help: some ideas might be how you treat others in some kind way; a special talent for drawing, dancing, saying funny things;

taking care of a pet or family member; or LOTS of other things. As we think about what we say to others, it's important to think about what we say to ourselves. Being kind works for both!

Good for you! You are noticing that each of you has a special skill or talent that makes you different from others. Isn't it nice that we all don't have to be alike, and we can enjoy our special gifts? Hint: It just might be that if you let someone else know that you notice his or her special talent, it will help you feel better about your own!

***

Next Is Story Six

Hannah the Hummingbird Teaching Tale (Assertiveness, Dependability)

Hannah, the ruby-throated hummingbird, had just finished her flight of over 1000 miles from Mexico, carrying only a tiny suitcase that held all her household needs for the summer ahead. She was tired and thirsty and had lost weight from some of her already very slim little body.

The busy little bird remembered the human who stocked her feeder outside of the house. She had been returning to The House for three summers and was impatient to see Marie and let her know that she was back in town. She was a few days early this year because the weather had been milder throughout her long flight. Unfortunately, Hannah didn't see the feeder out where it was usually placed.

She would have to look in the windows for some attention. Just as Hannah was about to fly around the house, she spotted Marie bent over in a flower bed, planting a few pink petunias. Hannah liked them but she needed a much longer drink than the young blooms could provide just now. She dived near Marie, hovering near her face, looking at her with the recognition of an old friend. Marie, hearing the roar of the fast-beating wings, looked up quickly wondering if she was being attacked, then smiled broadly to see her familiar little friend. Marie was amazed that her friend, as tiny as she was, remained so dependable that she returned to The House each year at about the same time to settle in for the summer.

Despite Hannah's dependability, Marie had neglected to get her hummingbird feeders ready this year. She would have to do that. Marie continued to plant in her flower bed and finally, Hannah moved a bit about the neighborhood looking for some nectar to drink to help with her thirst and hunger.

Determined to prompt Marie to get her feeders ready, Hannah returned to The House, flying to the windows to peer in the glass for Marie. As Hannah's parents had reminded her when she was even a tinier bird, if you want something badly enough, you might have to ask, and even ask again. Hannah had learned that lesson well. She was rewarded in a few minutes with a large hummingbird feeder placed near the window so that Marie could watch her and other little visitors as they sailed in, hovering for a drink.

Marie was embarrassed that such a tiny creature would remember her and needed to remind her of her "contract" for providing a feeder.

To avoid forgetting again next year, Marie put a note in the calendar on her phone and on her hanging calendar in the kitchen to remind her of when to expect Hannah next spring, so she wouldn't have to wait for her food next time.

Hannah the Hummingbird Talking Points:

- What do you think of Hannah the Hummingbird?

- How did Hannah finally get fed after her long trip?

- Would you say Hannah was too pushy or was she trying to be assertive (asking for what she needed)?

- While we often want others to do something that is not happening, we need to know how to be assertive, as opposed to being aggressive, when we would like for something to happen. An often-used technique for being assertive is the "broken-record technique." We ask for someone to do something; we explain how this would affect us in a good way, or how an action we want someone to stop has affected us in a bad way; then we repeat the request.

- Examples: Hannah Hummingbird asked assertively to be provided with her nectar. When she didn't get it and it was becoming a real necessity, she came back and asked again. Another example you might have personally experienced in school is the following. "I'd like for you to stop kicking my desk. When you kick it, it makes my books slide and I don't like that. Please stop kicking my desk." I'll bet you can think of an instance when you would like for someone to act differently around you!

- The important thing to realize is that we are unable to control what other people do, but in being assertive we are taking responsibility for asking for what we need in the world without being too pushy or too quiet. Often this approach builds our confidence, self-respect, and respect for others.

- What does being dependable mean? Who do you know who does things when they need to be done and whom you can trust to help you when necessary?

A bonus for mom and child: Over the next few days, how can you practice a broken record technique? You try too, Mom! Not pushy, but not too quiet? Asking for what you would like to happen. Explain how this would be helpful to you, or why you would like it to stop, then ask again. Remember that we can't control what other people do but we can explain what we would like to happen in the world and why. Then we can listen. Perhaps we will change our minds, or the other person will change theirs. If we get what we have asked for, then we can practice being thankful. Another way to think about the little story is to find a picture of a pretty hummingbird or think about stocking a feeder in the early spring throughout the summer. Any other ways?

Chapter 12: Deeper Personal Feelings

It's very normal to have mixed feelings about those we feel close to. Sometimes having what we think of as negative feelings about someone we love (such as anger, desire to be away from them, annoyance, impatience, or mistrust, for example) causes us to have feelings of guilt or discomfort. Exploring how we might hold seemingly conflicting feelings about someone is presented in the next simple, non-threatening story and might be enlightening and provide some relief if these conflicting feelings have been present for your little one.

Note that as a parent it's important to help your little one explore the question of when an uncomfortable feeling can be a warning to make a change in a relationship.

***

Get Ready for Story Seven

Release physical tension: Standing tall or seated with a straight spine, raise your shoulders to your ears and then release them back down. Do this a few times to release tension in your neck and upper back. Now, extend your arms straight out from your sides and turn your waist and arms from side to side a few times releasing tension in your waist and lower back areas. Remember to do only what is physically comfortable and approved by your physician if you have a health problem.

Focus Attention: Let's move like a porpoise. Seated or standing, allow your head to rest slightly forward as your straight arms meet stretched out in front of you. As you slowly inhale and extend your arms out to the side, raise your head and chin slightly. Exhale slowly, bringing your arms back together and gently lowering your head toward your chest. Slowly repeat this breath movement a few times as you settle your attention.

***

Calli, The Learning Teacher Teaching Tale (Forgiveness and Love)

Calli, the little gray, curly-haired dog who lives in The House was sitting quietly on the back stoop, watching the birds, and enjoying the afternoon. The neighborhood red squirrel scurried back and forth as it gathered acorns for fall. Noticing the quiet little dog, he stopped for a quick chat.

"Hi there. I'm Stevie. I was wondering what you do that allows you to live in The House with the humans there?"

Calli was pleased to have a new friend to talk to. "I'm a student and a teacher."

"What are you learning?" Stevie asked as his nose twitched quickly.

"I'm learning lots of words, like 'sit,' 'stay,' 'heel,' 'breakfast,' 'lunch,' 'supper,' and 'cookie.' I'm also learning how to raise my eyebrows, smile, and let my owner know I love her with a long, tender look in my eyes."

"Wow! That's a lot! What are you teaching?"

"Well," said Calli, "I'm teaching forgiveness and unconditional love."

"What does that mean?!" Stevie frowned.

"When my owner is grumpy and hurts my feelings with a harsh voice, I get quiet. Then I move close enough to her to touch her hand, leg, or body with my paw or my nose, and with my eyes, I tell her I love and forgive her."

"Why do you do that?! Maybe you could bite her instead, so she never is grumpy or harsh with you again!!"

Calli patiently explained, "No, you see the world is an angry place right now. Many people are being nasty and hurting others with their quick, mean revenge. But dogs are slowly evolving. (That means they are beginning to change as the world changes.) Dogs are learning forgiveness and love in order to better survive today. Our job is to help teach humans to do the same thing. As we teach humans forgiveness, we learn forgiveness even better!"

Stevie looked thoughtful for a moment before his furry tail quivered and he jumped to grab an acorn that fell. He shouted in his squeaky voice as he went, "Calli, good luck! I think you'll have a long and steady career!"

Calli the Learning Teacher Talking Points:
- Which character did you like best?

- What was Stevie like? (Curious, friendly, busy?)

- What was Calli like? (Quiet? Patient? Smart?)

- How difficult is it to forgive someone when they do something you don't like? Can you say more about that?

- I wonder if anyone has ever forgiven you for something you did in the past?

- If someone you care about upsets you, what can you do about that? (Talk to your mom or another adult you trust? Talk to the person who upset you if it wasn't something frightening?)

- If you care about someone, can you forgive them when they make a mistake? It will be helpful if you and your parent talk about someone's very serious mistakes involving physical harm or threat to you or another person. In the other milder direction, your parent can help you sort out your thoughts and feelings about someone saying something to hurt your feelings. Sometimes, while you can understand a person hurt you by mistake and you forgive them, it's also important to have trust that the person won't do it again. You might need an adult to help with this decision-making right now.

If someone upset you by their action and they were unaware of that, talking with them in a certain way can be helpful for both you and the person who upset you. (These are the steps of the broken record again):

"When you did________________ it upset me."

"I felt (sad, angry, hurt, lonely...)"

"I don't want you to do that again."

You might have to practice these steps a few times when you are upset so that you can say them calmly and surely to the person who upset you.

Even if the person doesn't apologize or agree they were in the wrong, you have stated how you felt because of what they said or did, and you explained how you would like the person to treat you in the future. That means that you are assertive and able to openly and calmly state how you see things, and that is a great quality to have!

Next Is Story Eight

***

Virginia and the Choir Teaching Tale (Seeing the Positive)

The evening was clearing, with some stars winking in the ink-black sky. A soft rain had fallen for a few hours before this, leaving water droplets sparkling like jewels on the grass in the soft light of The House.

The narrow stream nearby ran slowly with the recent rain. It was a lovely mild summer night, but the real magic was in the amazing chorus of frogs singing loudly together in a beautiful song, accented occasionally by the bass tones of a large bullfrog.

Sophie was a skinny 12-year-old girl with long dark braids, who was more at home outside than in. She looked at the trees at the end of the yard, heard the water and the singing of the frog chorus, and exclaimed to herself much louder than she intended, "What a great song!!"

Sophie heard a response in harmony with the rousing chorus, "We're glad you like it! Lots of folks complain about the rain, but we love it. It refreshes the Earth and gives us a deeper place to swim and lay our eggs. We love to celebrate Mother Nature and sing her praises! Our singing sometimes even helps us attract a mate!"

"Come croon along with us anytime," sang Virginia, and Sophie smiled widely and agreed she would, humming softly as she returned to The House.

Virginia and the Choir Talking Points:
- When have you complained about the rain or other types of weather?

- What reasons does "Mother Earth" have for the types of weather changes we see? Cool weather to give plants a rest? Snow to blanket the Earth, providing water for spring plants? Snow and ice for animals such as polar bears, arctic seals, and foxes? Cold weather for skunks and bears to have time to hibernate? Warm and hot weather to encourage growth? Rain for watering plants, providing drinking water, water for the fish and sea animals and sea plants? I'm sure you know more or can learn more.

- How did the frogs show they were thankful for the rain?

- What kind of weather do you like best? How do you feel when it's that kind of weather? How do you show you're thankful for that type of weather?

For a bonus and this one might be a challenge: If you choose to, you and/or your parent might think of ways to enjoy (at least a little) each kind of weather in your area, so that each day seems to bring a gift from Mother Earth.

SMILE! You're finding small ways to enjoy every day of the rest of your life.

CHAPTER 13: APPROPRIATE SELF REVELATION

As your communication and connection skills have improved throughout this book, the issues presented have become more complex. You and your young child have done a great job working together to enhance your relationship through:

- relaxing and focusing on one another for regular periods,

- using accepting and effective communication strategies to build increasing regard and trust in one another,

- developing memories of creatures and scenarios that will give you situations you can refer to and talk about in the future, and

- working on planning small projects to apply more concrete learning.

In these ways, you have developed an expanding spiral of communication and relationship that will serve you and your child for years to come, not only in your relationship but in extended social situations.

In this chapter, the teaching tale introduces more characters and issues. There are no individual solutions, but rather the process of resolving issues becomes the puzzle. It may be very interesting for you to see how your child responds to the situation presented and the characters involved. Based on the age of your child, you might wish to self-disclose an appropriate reaction of your own to the critter community issue, or to a similar learning experience you've had in a group setting. This can provide a powerful demonstration for your child that you can be trusted because you are human and brave. It allows you and your child to understand that you have your own experiences and opinions yet are willing and able to honor your child's unique outlook.

***

Get Ready for Story Nine

Release physical tension: Shake like a wet dog or kitty. Wiggle all over for a little while: hands, legs, head, arms, fingers! And don't forget to smile! Did that feel good?

Focus Attention: Now slow down. As you take a deep breath, pretend you are picking up a big, fragile soap bubble that you toss to your parent or little one. Play catch with one another for a few tosses as you breathe, move slowly, and gently toss and catch the bubble.

***

Critter Community Action Teaching Tale (Cooperation and Justice)

There was confusion, shrieking, anger, and fear in the neighborhood!! Two robins were darting about the cherry tree where they were nesting. Three crows were flying overhead, landing in the tall pines in between swoops to the ground, with loud raucous cawing, while they sounded the alarm. The dog, a border collie, in the yard next door, was running up and jumping on the fence, as it barked ferociously. A gray squirrel with a glorious fuzzy tail scurried back and forth on the ground, checking out the birds, and then hiding under the Weigela bushes. The community was up in arms! What or who was stirring up trouble?

A cowbird, the stocky black bird with a brown head, was trying to take over the robins' nest by pushing their unhatched eggs to the ground. GRAND THEFT AND ATTEMPTED MURDER! It was not to be tolerated!!

While the crows made sure the cowbird remained in the area, the well-regarded local turtle, its dark green-brown shell protecting wrinkled legs and neck, walked sedately out from beneath a Blue Spruce tree, wearing her glasses over her long rather hooked nose, and in distinguished low tones offered up a solution to the immediate chaos. "I am a neutral party here and am known for my careful decision-making and lack of overly quick action. If you wish, I will hear this case and recommend a reasonable solution for the wellbeing of the community." The cowbird looked a bit relieved as the calm turtle spoke, and the rest of the witnesses nodded in agreement.

Tatyana Turtle patiently and intently listened to the anxious and fearful story of the robin parents, the angry observations of the crows, and the versions of the local dog, squirrel, and other birds, including a bright-eyed little house wren.

She then asked the cowbird for a statement. "Ma'am," he said, "the cowbirds never learned to build nests themselves! We have always used other birds' nests! It's time for us to lay eggs and we need a place to stay."

Ms. T. Turtle thought for what seemed a very long time, her wrinkled face very serious, her glasses dropping further down on her nose. She finally responded, "Our world is changing. There is much violence and anger in the world that prompts us to make great and important changes in how we act and react to one another." She then stated firmly, "Our community cannot tolerate bullying, meanness, and violence to others. We all need to learn new ways of doing things and treating others to live peacefully and happily together." She slowly looked around at the gathering of community critters.

Immediately, the gray squirrel and the pretty house wren piped up and volunteered to teach the cowbird how to make a safe nest. With that news, Tatyana Turtle slowly spoke to the cowbird, "I strongly suggest you and your mate work with these two volunteers to learn nest-building. If you do learn nest-building, you may stay in the community and raise your family. If you choose to refuse, I advise you to move elsewhere and find an already abandoned nest."

The cowbird hesitantly spoke, "Thank you, Ma'am. I guess your suggestion sounds fair... We will work together and if this turns out

OK, we will raise our young ones here and teach them new nest-building skills when the time comes."

There was silence as everyone considered the outcome. With the "hearing" over, the neighborhood members returned to their day and thought about the new and changing world they were a part of. Would they be able to change as needed? Would their neighborhood remain safe and a pleasant place to be? They each hoped so.

Critter Community Action Talking Points:

- Who did you like best of all the community critters? What do you like about them?

- Why was everyone upset?

- What did you think of Ms. T's decision?

- Ms. T seemed very slow. I wonder why. (She asked for everyone's opinion? Thought about things for a while? Was concerned about the safety of the community? Other things?)

- Why do you think the community wanted Ms. T to decide about this community issue?

- What would you have done if you were a community critter?

- What do you think will happen next?

A bonus for parent and child for this teaching tale session:

How can you be a helpful member of your community in the next few days? Give someone a "second chance" to learn something like the cowbird, by teaching them how to do it? Draw a favorite character from the story and think about why they are so likable. Take your time like Ms. T to make an important decision. What else?

Chapter 14: Conclusion

I hope you and your little one have enjoyed conversing and connecting. Taking the time and making the opportunity to investigate stories that open conversations -- exploring and discussing, wondering, and savoring each other's experiences, thoughts, and feelings!

Success is usually assured through the repetition of important information. Many studies of habit change suggest that performing a new action for at least 21 days helps to establish a new behavior pattern.

If you are a busy, concerned parent who wants:

- to have an open and enduring relationship with your child,

- for your child to make sensible decisions,

- for your child to improve confidence and perform well socially and in school,

- for you and your family to have a well-balanced and informed life,

- then commit to interacting with your child regularly in a loving, attentive, curious manner. Enjoy the unique qualities of your child and observe changes that might prompt you to explore new developments and experiences in your child's life that would benefit from your attention.

You can do this!! You're on your way to becoming more aware of your standards for being a human and a parent in an ever-changing world. And you are developing an inviting climate, setting, and vocabulary of images, characters, themes, actions, and ideas that provide you and your child with a way to discuss life issues and develop a sense of how and why they are important to you. In simpler terms, you are enhancing the richness of problem-solving with your child and perhaps even creating ways the two of you seek to improve your positive impact on the world!

Bonus Stories

As a bonus for completing this workbook and working on the **4stepsconnect** process of stretching, focusing, communicating effectively, and engaging, I hope you will enjoy a few bonus teaching tales. These are complete with the stretching, focusing, and talking points structure to further your expanding spiral of communication and relationship with your child.

***

Get Ready for Bonus Story One

Release physical tension: Let's work on Lion. Often our facial muscles get tense when we're out in public during the day. We might be smiling a lot and trying to appear pleasant, or we become serious-looking, attempting to appear that we are paying attention. It's nice to be able to simply stretch our facial muscles and have a bit of fun doing it while also stretching our vocal cords, the area that helps us make loud noises.

Take a big slow inhale while closing your eyes. As you open your eyes wide and roll them skywards, bring your hands in front of your chest as if they are lion's claws as you open your mouth wide, stick out your tongue, and growl, "Haa!!" Take a few breaths and try the whole movement again. Next time you might move your tongue to the left or right side of your mouth while you growl. Don't forget to enjoy yourself being a lion for a few moments.

Focus attention: Take a moment to slow down now. Take a few deep breaths down into your belly and release them through the soles of your feet, as you say to yourself, "I am relaxed and ready to focus my attention now."

***

Beautiful Merrybelle Teaching Tale (Beauty)

The stunning blue butterfly flitted among the flowers and shrubs at the front porch of The House before she landed on a day lily for a long drink. She was sunbathing on the warm, sunny brick sidewalk as Ann, who lived in The House, walked outside to check the view. The view she saw included spotting the butterfly's dazzling black to deep blue shaded wings, highlighted with small white spots, slowly moving up and down.

"Ooh," she said. "You're gorgeous!"

Merrybelle, the butterfly, introduced herself and responded, "Thank you so much!"

Anne asked her lovely visitor how long she would be staying. Merrybelle slowly opened and closed her wings as she soaked up the sun and explained, "I won't be here long, just enough time to spread pops of beauty and wonder around the neighborhood, as I've shown to you. I'll also help spread pollen among the flowers so they will continue to provide nectar for my butterfly friends for years to come." She added, "It's nice to be here with you because you have flowers, herbs, and some decayed wood in the field behind The House that I can eat while I work. And you also have a small pool where I can drink! I hope you continue to have those for the butterflies who follow me."

Ann's eyes grew wide as she watched the butterfly preen and stretch. "I wish I could spread beauty through the world like you do."

"Oh, but you can, Ann! Share your smile with others as you have with me, and you will show your beautiful spirit and inspiration to the world. This will help the human folks know that there is beauty everywhere, especially inside themselves. That important information has been lost over time."

Ann considered Merrybelle's comments and decided that she could certainly try to smile more and thought perhaps this might help her recognize the beauty she'd kept hidden from others and herself for quite some time.

Beautiful Merrybelle Talking Points:

- I wonder if there is anything you like about Merrybelle?

- If so, what do you like about her? (Pretty? Nice?)

- What does she add to the rest of the world? (Happiness? Beauty? Encouragement? Politeness? Cleans up the environment? Spreads pollen for butterflies and flowers?)

- Does Merrybelle believe that you must be beautiful on the outside to spread beauty in the world? What do you think?

- Do you know of someone that you think spreads beauty through his or her smile, actions, or way of treating others? If you do, it might be nice to let that person know, if that feels comfortable.

- How can you spread beauty and encouragement in the world? (Smile? Plant flowers for the butterflies?)

- What kind of flowers do butterflies like?

I'm glad you and your parent read and covered the topic of this story. Very often we hear from a lot of different people or news sources that beauty is what we see, usually modeled by what we see in magazines, or on TV. Hopefully, as you've discussed Merrybelle, you've learned that beauty can be on the outside, but beauty is also in our actions and how we treat others and the environment. We <u>all</u> can choose to be beautiful (or handsome if that feels better to you), and that's an important idea if we want to make a positive difference in the world.

For a bonus maybe there is an action you and/or your parent plan to take to spread more beauty in the world this week. Some ideas might include smiling at someone you don't know well, planting a flower in the yard, carefully picking up a bit of trash during your morning walk, or posting a pretty butterfly picture on your refrigerator door.

What can you think of?

***

Get Ready for Bonus Story Two

Release physical tension: Let's stretch like a cat and then like a cow. Standing and placing your hands just above your knees raise your head and chin as you roll your shoulders back and stick your belly out ("cow"), then keeping your hands just above your knees, roll your head forward and chin down rolling your back up and drawing your tummy in like an angry cat. Slowly shift from cow and cat, gently stretching your back and neck. This can be done seated if standing is not a healthful idea for you.

Focus attention: Since we're focusing on animals in this phase, let's try "humming bee breath." In a seated position, use your thumbs to gently press the tragus, the tiny flap at the opening of your ear canal to close your ears, while using your fingers to gently cover your eyes. Take a full breath and hum, finding that the hum sounds a bit like a bee and that you're focused fully on your humming sound rather than the sights or sounds around you. Use several breaths and hums. Students have reported that this technique helps them calm and get ready to study for an exam or other stressful chore.

***

Cassandra the Snake Teaching Tale (Awareness of Danger)

The large-sized (30" long) garden snake was lying still on the hot sunny edge of the macadam street, running through the neighborhood where Betty, the brightly colored Blue Jay lived. Betty, always interested in the news, looked more closely at Cassandra, the snake, and noticed her trembling a bit every few seconds. Being a curious and somewhat aggressive bird, Betty swooped down next to Cassandra and asked, "What's the matter?! Why are you crying?"

Cassandra, crying a bit from fear and hurt feelings, finally answered through her sniffles. "People are afraid of me and don't like me because I'm a snake. That car that went by tried to run over me, but I was able to get away! I'm not so bad, you know. I'm not poisonous. I don't kill people and I try to keep to myself. You know, I'm helpful by eating mice and other rodents that can be harmful to people and their property."

Betty who was a bit loud and brash tried to be understanding and help Cassandra calm down. "Well, I don't understand. If you're not dangerous, why are people afraid of you and hate you so much?"

In talking to her chatty listener, Cassandra began to feel better and to think things through a bit. "You know Betty, I have a more important job in life that might seem a bit strange..."

"What's that?" Betty asked, jerking her head sharply forward to avoid missing a word.

Cassandra responded, "Some snakes are very dangerous. They are poisonous and can kill people or other animals, or at least make them very sick. Some large snakes can and do eat very large animals. The thing is, it's not easy to quickly tell which snakes are dangerous and which are not. Parents teach their children to be afraid of snakes, avoid them and tell their parents if they see one. This is for children's safety. In a way, snakes remind people that it's not always easy to tell what or who might be dangerous to them."

Cassandra continued, "Sometimes there are dangers when things look nice and safe. While it's not good to always be looking for something bad to happen because we want to have a joy-filled life, it's important to be very observant and cautious."

Betty fluttered her wings a bit and strutted close to Cassandra, "Is the moral of your story to be careful of what you might step on or pick up?"

Cassandra managed a little smile, responding, "You bet!"

Cassandra the Snake Talking points:

- What do you tend to be afraid of?

- What have you found out about these things? That they are dangerous? Maybe not so dangerous all the time?

- What do you notice that helps you decide if something or

someone is dangerous or not good to be around?

- What can you think of that seemed fine, but turned out to be hurtful to you? Poison ivy? Bumble bees? A food that you're allergic to? A person who was hurtful to you or bullied you?

- It would be sad to be labeled as "not nice" if that weren't true. I wonder if you know of anyone who has been bothered in that way.

***

Get ready for Bonus Story Three

Release physical tension: Let's release tension in our hands and wrists. We often have tense hands by the end of the day, from typing, texting, twisting, grasping, gardening, and carrying. First, squeeze your fingers in, then release them straight out, stretching to knead like a cat does when he's happy. Squeeze in, then straighten out long for a few times. After that, roll your hands around your wrists, first one way and then the other way a few times. As you roll your wrists, raise your arms up and down, shake your hands, and smile.

Focus attention: As we breathe gently, we're going to move our eyes slowly around an imaginary clock face. Raise your eyes to the top of the clock (12), then slowly circle to 1,2,3,4,5,6. At this point, your eyes will be looking down.

Then continue to circle from 6,7,8,9,10,11, and back to 12. Make that circle twice. Continue to breathe gently and circle your eyes slowly in the opposite direction around the clock. When you finish that backward circle two times, rub your hands together until they are warm, then hold your palms loosely and tenderly over your eyes for a few slow breaths. Lower your hands and tell yourself you are ready to focus and pay attention.

***

Robin the Recycler Teaching Tale (Caring for the Environment)

Mr. and Mrs. Robin, the Recyclers, were collecting items for the nest they were building in the backyard of The House.

The Robins were gathering twigs and grasses that had blown through the yard during the winter.

Mr. Robin found a piece of twine from some packaging and was taking it to their nesting project. Both Robins were very busy searching for items for their new home.

Marcus, who lived in The House, entered the yard with a basket and rake. He was assigned to clean up the stray leaves, branches, and wayward trash that found its way there during the windy winter weather.

Noticing Mr. Robin carrying the twine in his beak, Marcus said, "You don't have to use that old stuff for your nest, I have some nice cloth pieces I used for a school project, and my mom has some new green yarn stashed in her desk, that she never uses."

Mr. Robin responded, "That's very kind of you, but we like to recycle, by using things that others don't care about anymore and throw away."

Ms. Robin overheard the conversation and flitted closer. "I like to look for little treasures while we're recovering used items. I just found some sparkly ribbon that will make our new nest very pretty. Her eyes twinkled as she exclaimed, "When we recycle, every nest we build is a one-of-a-kind work of art!"

Robin the Recycler Talking Points:

- What do you think about the Robins who recycle?

- How was Marcus trying to help?

- I wonder if there are any items you could reuse differently? Small pieces of colored paper or ribbon that you could use for a school or art project? Could clothes that you outgrow be used for someone younger?

Bonus project: In the next week, you and your parent might think of something you could recycle -- for example, taking your plastic grocery bags to a market that collects them to be made into something else. When you brush your pet, you might gather the pet hair from the brush and place it in a quiet spot in the backyard, where it won't blow. Birds and small animals could use this for their nests. If you have a favorite blanket that's worn and has been replaced, you might take your old one to an animal shelter to be used in the kennels there.

What can you think of that might be re-used differently?

You are terrific! You and your child are creating memories and connections that will positively serve you as you grow together in experience and understanding.

Both of you have begun a journey to becoming relaxed, attentive, thoughtful, and engaged listeners who confidently and compassionately interact with one another and the world.

REFERENCES AND RESOURCES

"The Art of Impactful Storytelling," Dr. Jean Houston, <u>The Influencers Masterclass</u> online,

Dr. Claire Zammit and Dr. Jean Houston, 2022.

"How to Communicate Effectively with Your Young Child," Unicef, 11/8/22.

"The Power of Storytelling," Clare Patey and Cathy Irving, The Health Foundation, 12/12/2016,

https://www.health.org.uk/newsletter-feature/power-ofstorytelling.

<u>Raising Good Humans</u>, Hunter Clarke-Fields, MSAE, New Harbinger Publications, Inc., 2019.

Responsive Classroom, National Coalition for Parental Involvement in Education, 2006.

"7 Tips for Communicating with Your School-aged Child," Gary Gilles, https://mentalhelp.net, 11/8/22.

<u>Stolen Focus</u>, Johann Hari, Crown Publishing, 2022.

<u>Therapists Guide to Clinical Intervention</u>, Sharon L. Johnson, Academic Press, 1997.

"What Makes Storytelling So Effective for Learning?" Vanessa Boris, 12/20/2017, https://www.harvardbusiness.org.

"Young Children and Communication," Better Health Channel, 11/8/22.

Photos in the book are from the author's collection and Pixabay free stock photos

Thank You

T hank you for reading this book!

I want to share the book with as many people as possible. If you found this book helpful, entertaining, or inspiring, I would greatly appreciate your leaving me a review. Your review helps others find the book as well.

Be well and take care, my friend.

Suanne

DISCLAIMER

This document is intended to provide exact and reliable information on the topic and issue covered. The publication is sold based on the idea that the publisher is not required to render an accounting, officially permitted, or otherwise, of qualified services. If advice is necessary, legal, financial, medical, or professional, a practiced individual in the profession should be ordered.

This information is not presented by a financial or medical practitioner and is for entertainment, educational and informational purposes only. The content is not intended as a substitute for professional medical advice, diagnosis, or treatment. Always seek the advice of your physician or other qualified healthcare provider with any questions you may have regarding a medical condition. Never disregard professional medical advice or delay in seeking it because of something you have read.

The information provided herein is stated to be truthful and consistent, in that any liability, in terms of inattention or otherwise, by any usage or abuse of any policies, processes, or directions contained within is the solitary and utter responsibility of the recipient reader.

 DR. SUANNE LEWIS

Under no circumstances will any legal responsibility or blame be held against the publisher for any reparation, damages, or monetary loss due to the information herein, either directly or indirectly.

OTHER BOOKS BY THE AUTHOR

BAXTER TALES: Personally Transformed By A Basset Hound Who Taught Me About Coping with Change

Do you ever feel like life is moving too fast, leaving you feeling overwhelmed and struggling to cope with the changes it brings? Perhaps you've tried all sorts of self-help books and strategies, but nothing seems to stick.

Well, I'm here to tell you about a book that just might change everything. Introducing "BAXTER TALES: Personally Transformed by A Basset Hound Who Taught Me About Coping with Change," available in ebook, paperback, and audible versions.

"BAXTER TALES" will help you:

– Embrace change and uncertainty with grace and confidence
– Cultivate resilience in the face of adversity
– Strengthen your relationships and connections with others
– Find joy and meaning in the small moments of everyday life

Whether you're a dog lover, a self-help enthusiast, or just someone looking for a little inspiration and guidance, "BAXTER TALES" has something for you. The author's honest and vulnerable writing style will make you feel like you're sitting down for coffee with a trusted friend, and Baxter's adorable antics will leave you smiling and uplifted.

So what are you waiting for? Order your copy of "BAXTER TALES" today. You won't regret it - we promise.

About the Author

Dr. Suanne Lewis is a psychologist, author, accredited T'ai Chi Chih and Yoga instructor, wife, mother, and dog enthusiast!

For additional information about her upcoming projects, contact her at: drsuanne@4stepsconnect.com

Free Download: "Unlocking Mindfulness: 10 Techniques for a Balanced Life"

Are you ready to discover the transformative power of mindfulness? Whether you're new to mindfulness or looking to deepen your practice, our free guide is your gateway to a more balanced and fulfilling life.

In "Unlocking Mindfulness," you'll explore ten mindfulness techniques, each designed to help you stretch your potential, focus your mind, communicate effectively, and fully engage in the present moment. "Unlocking Mindfulness" explores ten mindfulness techniques that harness the power of these four core principles.

This free guide will empower you with the knowledge and practices to:

Stretch for Serenity

- Discover simple stretching exercises that release tension, increase flexibility, and prepare your mind and body for mindfulness.

Focus for Clarity

- Develop the art of focused attention, enabling you to sharpen your concentration, reduce distractions, and enhance decision-making.

Communicate Effectively for Improved Relationships

- Learn the keys to mindful communication, including active listening, and empathy, leading to improved relationships.

Engage for a Fulfilling Life

- Understand the importance of fully engaging in your daily activities, bringing a deeper sense of joy and purpose into your life.

With this guide, you'll gain practical insights, tips, and exercises that will help you:

Reduce stress and anxiety Boost emotional intelligence Cultivate focus and attention Enhance your overall well-being

Begin your mindfulness journey today and experience its positive impact on your life and relationships. Download our free guide now and take the first step towards a more balanced and peaceful existence.

To claim your free copy of "Unlocking Mindfulness," email us, and we'll send it to your inbox:

EMAIL drsuanne@4stepsconnect.com

Simply indicate "Free copy. "

Include your first name and email address.

Start your journey toward greater well-being and mindfulness mastery today. Download your free guide now!